30 DAY
RETURN TO PLAY
JOURNAL

An Edge in Sports, Mental Reps for Life

· Priscilla Tallman, MS Clinical Psychology ·

30 Day Return to Play Journal

© Copyright 2020, Priscilla Tallman, MS Clinical Psychology

ISBN: 978-1-950892-74-7

www.spikedr.com

 @pytallman

 pytallman@gmail.com

Journal design by Esther BeLer Wodrich. www.estherbeler.com

Cover photo by Connor Coyne on Unsplash

The injury cycle has stopped many great athletic careers in their tracks, and not always because of a permanent physical limitation. I've been on both sides of the injury spectrum as an athlete and as Strength Coach and Physical Therapist. I've rehabbed countless patients and athletes and had to be the empathetic observer as well as the athlete experiencing the injury so I know being injured is a frustrating journey. From the moment of injury to the clinic and back to your arena, we are always looking for another tool to arm our patients with for the long journey back. There is mounting literature and loads of clinical experience pointing to daily mindset and mental resilience work as one of the most important tools for athletes returning to play. This mental resilience is not always easy and definitely not second nature - you have to train it. I can't say enough what a gift it is that someone with Priscilla's experience has put together a tool to arm our patients in such a time of need.

Will Trujillo, DPT, OCS, FAFS

Welcome athlete! When I work with athletes from various levels of different sports – from club to high school to college and beyond – one of the biggest fears/risks associated with playing the sport they love is getting an injury.

Why? Because it means a temporary hold on our sport and shift of focus away from our team and individual goals to focusing on getting our bodies and minds back to a place where we can be competitive again.

If you haven't already heard, **journaling is a powerful mindset tool**. Research in this area supports that journaling not only helps clarify your thoughts and feelings, it can also reduce cortisol (stress hormone) levels, lead to more effective problem solving skills and promote healthy forms of communications with others such as those found in team environments.

Physical injury isn't the only reason playing your can be put on hold. Mental illness such as depression or anxiety is becoming a more common reason student-athletes take time off to get help. In fact, recent data shows that up to 35% of elite athletes suffer from a mental health crisis at some point in their career. Major illness, family emergency or other outside circumstances can also lead to time off from sport.

This journal will walk you through valuable mental reps while you work on getting back physically as well. In just 30 days, you will become more aware of your thoughts, learn visualization skills, stop comparing or critiquing your progress **so you can focus on getting back to the competition arena and back to doing what you love.**

Priscilla Tallman, MS Clinical Psychology
Performance and Mindset Coach

INSTRUCTIONS

The **30 Day Return to Play Journal** is designed to progress you through 30 days of journal prompts as you work through being sidelined. Research supports that journaling can help reduce cortisol levels which can lead to reduced inflammation. In addition, it has been linked to increased serotonin and dopamine levels which can also promote an elevated mood during a time when you are separated from your sport.

If you are feeling more than just a little down about being sidelined by an injury or otherwise find yourself isolating and removing yourself completely from friends, family and mentors, see APPENDIX C for additional resources. Remember, many athletes have navigated the difficult time after an injury and you are not alone. Reach out to a coach, mentor, friend, trainer or PT and stay connected.

Pre and Post Game Huddle are assessments that will measure your growth over the 30 days of journaling. Journaling is a habit, so as you work through your 30 days, you are creating a new mindset habit as well. Before starting "Day 1," fill out the Pre-Game Huddle assessment. Be as honest as you can. After "Day 28", complete the Post-Game Huddle assessment at the end of the journal. Compare the first assessment to the second one and see where you made improvements. Where did you improve? Is there anything that stayed the same? Are there areas where you could use more work?

Each day includes work that primes your brain for learning. This section is on the left side of the page and is called **PRIME TIME** (yeah, it's named after one of my favorite athletes). It looks like this:

1: **What's In the Tank?** — Learning how to accurately and honestly assess your emotions and mood on any give day is a valuable life skill that creates self-awareness. The number isn't to predict how your day will go, it's an honest look at your mood. The idea here is to take what's currently in the tank and move it one or two clicks forward if it's low or figure out how to use that full tank when you have it.

2: **Recharge** — No matter where your tank stands, learning the mindset skill of gratitude is important. Like journaling, gratitude work has been shown to decrease cortisol levels and increase serotonin and dopamine. Some days you gotta dig for something to be thankful for, but you can be thankful for even the smallest wins when you look closely.

3: **Visualization** — Rehearsing your comeback, imagining your first day back on the field, connecting to your emotions about what it feels like to put on that jersey for the first time after your setback; all of these things can be rehearsed with visualization or imagery work. See APPENDIX A for additional information.

TABLE OF CONTENTS

Rate yourself for each question below using this scale:

1   **2**   **3**   **4**

nope   *meh*   *sometimes*   *100%*

I journal regularly   _____

I believe journaling is a valuable mental skill   _____

I am open to feedback   _____

I apply feedback well   _____

I ask questions to learn   _____

I believe the mental game is as important   _____
as the physical game

I work hard on my mental game   _____

I have been told I "get in my head"   _____

I get down on myself as an athlete   _____

I bounce back after setbacks and mistakes   _____

My coach inspires and motivates me   _____

THE TRANSITION

"I'm not the same athlete"

When you are sidelined for any reason, you aren't physically in the arena. You worry about how long you'll be out, you feel like a different athlete than you were before the injury and will your spot still be there when you return? This section will inspire your recovery work and remind you to keep it one day at a time as your body heals.

PRIME TIME

➡️ *Assess.*

What's in the tank? Draw an arrow to how full your energy tank is right now.

½   E   F

➡️ *Recharge.*

Something I am grateful for today:

My parents and sibling for their constant support

Someone I am grateful for today:

My sister

One piece of advice I'd give a teammate if they were in my situation:

Try not to think so much and just play

➡️ *Visualize.* Spend a few minutes imagining your favorite sports play. This can be a moment when you were your happiest, most fulfilled or having an amazing game. The key here is to choose a moment where you were doing something well. Add as much detail as possible including sights, sounds, emotions, colors, etc.

First things first.

In order to progress, you're gonna have to keep your eyes on your own paper. Your progress is your progress. No one else can do this work but you.

We cool? *Ok, let's get started.*

◻ My **NAME** is: Georgia Fusco

◻ My **FAVORITE THING** about sports is: being able to go to the beach everyday

◻ One **SPECIFIC GOAL** I'd like to attain in 30 Days is:

Practice consicistancy → be able to play consistantly

◻ One **MEASUREABLE GOAL** I'd like to attain in 30 Days is: Well

Be lifting the same or more than I was, when I left

◻ One **ATTAINABLE GOAL** I'd like to meet in 30 Days is:

Hit more cut shots

◻ One **REALISTIC GOAL** I'd like to meet in 30 Days is:

feel game ready to do my two step

◻ One **TIME SPECIFIC GOAL** I'd like to meet in 30 Days is:

Go to bed before 11 on practice nights

❙ PRO TIP: This is called **S.M.A.R.T goal setting** (George T. Doran).

5

PRIME TIME

→ *Assess.*
What's in the tank? Draw an arrow to how full your energy tank is right now.

→ *Recharge.*
Something I am grateful for today:

The opportunity to play at such a great school

Someone I am grateful for today:

Betsi

One piece of advice I'd give a teammate if they were in my situation:

Find joy when you play

→ *Visualize.* Spend a few minutes imagining your favorite sports play. This can be a moment when you were your happiest, most fulfilled or having an amazing game. The key here is to choose a moment where you were doing something well. Add as much detail as possible including sights, sounds, emotions, colors, etc.

"I've crashed many, many times, just this one tore my knee apart. But crashing is part of my sport - if you can't get over it, then you should probably stop skiing."

–Lindsey Vonn: The Climb

Being sidelined by an injury gives us time. Time we'd rather spend training for our sport; but training our minds is just as valuable (if not more) to our game as our physical training. In the columns below write down what has changed since your injury and what has stayed the same.

WHAT'S THE SAME?	WHAT'S CHANGED?
Same people	on campus court
Same coaches	playing w/ masks
Same balls	no high fives
Same game	have more anxiety

PRO TIP: Watch "Lindsey Vonn: The Climb" on Red Bull TV

PRIME TIME

➡ *Assess.*

What's in the tank? Draw an arrow to how full your energy tank is right now.

½

E

F

◉

➡ *Recharge.*

Something I am grateful for today:

_____

_____

Someone I am grateful for today:

_____

_____

One piece of advice I'd give a teammate if they were in my situation:

_____

_____

➡ *Visualize.* Spend a few minutes imagining your favorite sports play. This can be a moment when you were your happiest, most fulfilled or having an amazing game. The key here is to choose a moment where you were doing something well. Add as much detail as possible including sights, sounds, emotions, colors, etc.

Establish a daily routine. ROUTINES are based around the rising and setting of the sun. They are more flexible than hourly schedules. It's okay to not have a schedule that works for you just yet, but getting into a routine is important for your body to heal and to keep you anchored so that you can create good habits.

Example **MORNING**
6:00am Wake Up
6:30am Breakfast
7:00am Get Dressed

MORNING ☀	EVENING 🌙
_____	_____
_____	_____
_____	_____
_____	_____
_____	_____

* where does this journal time fit into your routine?

> **PRO TIP:** Track your meal times (not *what* you eat, just *when* you eat). Try to eat around the same time everyday to get your body and digestion on a steady routine.

PRIME TIME

➜ *Assess.*
What's in the tank? Draw an arrow to how full your energy tank is right now.

½

E

F

➜ *Recharge.*
Something I am grateful for today:

_____

_____

Someone I am grateful for today:

_____

_____

One piece of advice I'd give a teammate if they were in my situation:

_____

_____

➜ *Visualize.* Spend a few minutes imagining your favorite sports play. This can be a moment when you were your happiest, most fulfilled or having an amazing game. The key here is to choose a moment where you were doing something well. Add as much detail as possible including sights, sounds, emotions, colors, etc.

As you work towards rebuilding your strength physically, think about what habits are going to get you there. You may have some habits already established, but you'll need some new ones too so your body and mind can heal and grow stronger, more resilient.

(Circle) all that apply and add your own. Start at the base of the triangle with habits that give you a strong foundation, work your way up to a goal at the top of the triangle.

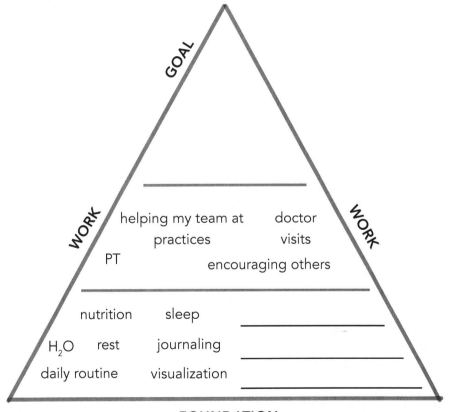

GOAL

WORK

WORK

helping my team at practices   doctor visits

PT

encouraging others

nutrition   sleep   _____

H$_2$O   rest   journaling   _____

daily routine   visualization   _____

FOUNDATION

PRO TIP: Don't try to change everything at once. Start with one small daily habit and work from there. Add one habit you want to improve or remove a habit – either one leads to change.

11

PRIME TIME

➡️ *Assess.*
What's in the tank? Draw an arrow to how full your energy tank is right now.

½

E   F

➡️ *Recharge.*
Something I am grateful for today:

_____

_____

Someone I am grateful for today:

_____

_____

One piece of advice I'd give a teammate if they were in my situation:

_____

_____

➡️ *Visualize.* Spend a few minutes imagining your favorite sports play. This can be a moment when you were your happiest, most fulfilled or having an amazing game. The key here is to choose a moment where you were doing something well. Add as much detail as possible including sights, sounds, emotions, colors, etc.

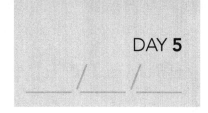

"I started thinking about who I am off the floor. I started searching for what success is outside of basketball. If I didn't play sports again, what could I possible do that still brings value to the world and to my family?"

–Anna Wilson, Stanford Basketball

Our identity as an athlete is different from our value as an athlete. In the chart below, (circle) those things that have meaning to you from both columns. Read APPENDIX B after completing this day.

🏃 Athlete IDENTITY	♡ Athlete VALUE
FOLLOWERS / LIKES	MY WORK ETHIC
LEADER	I CONTRIBUTE TO A TEAM
ROLE MODEL	I'M A LEADER
POPULAR ON CAMPUS	I LOVE MY TEAM/FAMILY
BEING ON A WINNING TEAM	I INVEST IN MY FUTURE
I'M A GOOD ATHLETE	I HANDLE ADVERSITY
COOL MERCH	I CAN ADAPT IN ALL SITUATIONS
PEOPLE KNOW ME	I'M RELIABLE
WHEN THE CROWD CHEERS	I'M DEPENDABLE
MAKE MY SCHOOL PROUD	I'M DETERMINED.
MAKE MY FAMILY PROUD	I CAN PERSEVERE IN HARD TIMES
	I AM A LOYAL TEAMMATE

PRIME TIME

➡️ *Assess.*

What's in the tank? Draw an arrow to how full your energy tank is right now.

E   ½   F

➡️ *Recharge.*

Something I am grateful for today:

_____

_____

Someone I am grateful for today:

_____

_____

One piece of advice I'd give a teammate if they were in my situation:

_____

_____

➡️ *Visualize.* Spend a few minutes imagining your favorite sports play. This can be a moment when you were your happiest, most fulfilled or having an amazing game. The key here is to choose a moment where you were doing something well. Add as much detail as possible including sights, sounds, emotions, colors, etc.

"I was really tired, man. Just tired in the locker room, upset and dejected and thinking about this … mountain to overcome. I mean, this is a long process. I wasn't sure I could do it,"

-Kobe Bryant of his achilles injury

It is common to feel "separate" or isolated from your team while you work to get back on the field or court or track. It's also important to share your thoughts with people we trust.

WHO are some people I trust with my thoughts or struggles?

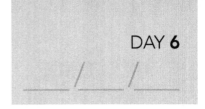

_____

_____

WHAT is one physical thing I'm struggling with today?

_____

_____

WHAT is one mental thing I'm struggling with today?

_____

_____

15

PRIME TIME

→ *Assess.*
What's in the tank? Draw an arrow to how full your energy tank is right now.

½

E   F

⊙

→ *Recharge.*
Something I am grateful for today:

_____

_____

Someone I am grateful for today:

_____

_____

One piece of advice I'd give a teammate if they were in my situation:

_____

_____

→ *Visualize.* Spend a few minutes imagining your favorite sports play. This can be a moment when you were your happiest, most fulfilled or having an amazing game. The key here is to choose a moment where you were doing something well. Add as much detail as possible including sights, sounds, emotions, colors, etc.

WEEKLY RECAP – THE TRANSITION

"I came back after my surgery throwing four to six miles harder than I did before"

-Curt Schilling

Write down **three** high points from this week (can be from any area of your life).

_____

_____

_____

Two things I learned from journaling this week are:

_____

_____

One habit I created and stuck to this week is:

_____

| **PRO TIP:** You are one week into creating a new habit. Keep going, keep making your journal a priority.

THE TRAP
COMPARISON
COMPARISON

One of the biggest traps of progressing after an injury (or otherwise) is comparing your progress or your timeline to someone else. It's crazy to think we all have different injuries and different goals, but we still have this tendency to compare ourselves to other athletes. This section will give you tools to help focus your attention on your own work and your own progress so you can chase your own goals and not get distracted by someone else's goals.

PRIME TIME

→ *Assess.*
What's in the tank? Draw an arrow to how full your energy tank is right now.

½

E   F

⊙

→ *Recharge.*
Something I am grateful for today:

_____

_____

Someone I am grateful for today:

_____

_____

One piece of advice I'd give a teammate if they were in my situation:

_____

_____

→ *Visualize.* Spend a few minutes imagining your favorite sports play. This can be a moment when you were your happiest, most fulfilled or having an amazing game. The key here is to choose a moment where you were doing something well. Add as much detail as possible including sights, sounds, emotions, colors, etc.

___ / ___ / ___

"Why waste time proving over and over how great you are when you could be getting better,"

–Carol Dweck

Comparison can lead your thoughts astray and distract you from your own progress. Spend some time improving your thoughts by investigating the following truths.

My **truth** as an athlete TODAY is:

_____

_____

_____

I am **the kind of athlete** who:

_____

_____

_____

It is **like me** to:

_____

_____

_____

_____

PRO TIP: When you feel like comparing yourself to someone else this week, come back to these truths and remember your truth as an athlete.

PRIME TIME

➡ *Assess.*
What's in the tank? Draw an arrow to how full your energy tank is right now.

½

E   F

◉

➡ *Recharge.*
Something I am grateful for today:

_____

_____

Someone I am grateful for today:

_____

_____

One piece of advice I'd give a teammate if they were in my situation:

_____

_____

➡ *Visualize.* Spend a few minutes imagining your favorite sports play. This can be a moment when you were your happiest, most fulfilled or having an amazing game. The key here is to choose a moment where you were doing something well. Add as much detail as possible including sights, sounds, emotions, colors, etc.

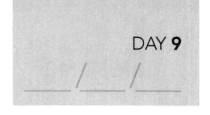

/ /

"Every action you take is a vote for the type of person you wish to become"

-James Clear, **Atomic Habits**

We've all seen the image of the iceberg in the ocean. The top (the smaller part) represents what people see and the bottom (the larger part) represents the foundation and the things people don't see. Take this time to show what actions you are taking that no one sees. What work are you doing that feels small, but is building a solid base for your future self?

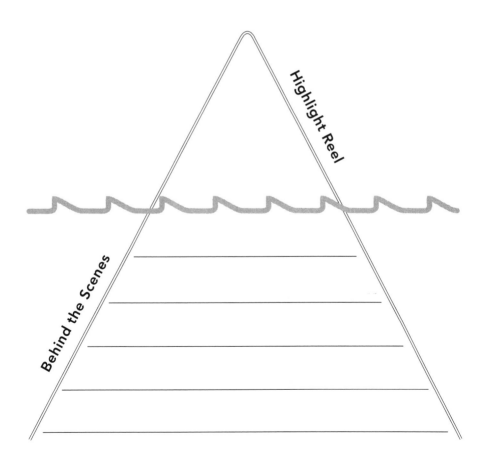

23

PRIME TIME

➡ *Assess.*
What's in the tank? Draw an arrow to how full your energy tank is right now.

➡ *Recharge.*
Something I am grateful for today:

_____

_____

Someone I am grateful for today:

_____

_____

One piece of advice I'd give a teammate if they were in my situation:

_____

_____

➡ *Visualize.* Spend a few minutes imagining your favorite sports play. This can be a moment when you were your happiest, most fulfilled or having an amazing game. The key here is to choose a moment where you were doing something well. Add as much detail as possible including sights, sounds, emotions, colors, etc.

_____ / _____ / _____

"There's only so dark a hole you can put yourself in and I just was worried I wouldn't be able to pull myself back out,"

–Lindsey Vonn: The Climb

Comparison can lead to strong emotions. Sometimes those feelings sneak up on us when we least expect it. **Draw an arrow** to those emotions you have felt during your recovery time.

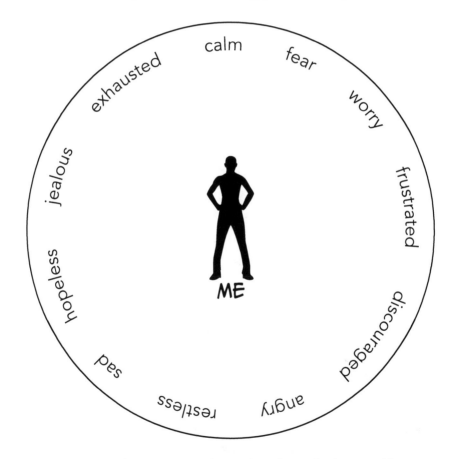

These are normal emotions to have, but if you find yourself in more than a temporary rut, find a friend, physical therapist, coach, parent or trainer to talk to. (See APPENDIX C & D)

PRIME TIME

➡ *Assess.*
What's in the tank? Draw an arrow to how full your energy tank is right now.

➡ *Recharge.*
Something I am grateful for today:

_____

_____

Someone I am grateful for today:

_____

_____

One piece of advice I'd give a teammate if they were in my situation:

_____

_____

➡ *Visualize.* Spend a few minutes imagining your favorite sports play. This can be a moment when you were your happiest, most fulfilled or having an amazing game. The key here is to choose a moment where you were doing something well. Add as much detail as possible including sights, sounds, emotions, colors, etc.

/ /

We can't avoid all comparison, but we can put ourselves in healthy environments that lift our mood. Identifying people, places and time of day is important so you know where to look when you need a boost in energy, morale or motivation. Let's identify these now so we can use them later in the journal when we work on visualization.

3 **places where my mind is in a good place**
& I can focus on my progress

_____

_____

_____

2 **places I can plug in to my team**
with no judgement

_____

_____

1 **place that is a distraction**
or brings me down

_____

PRIME TIME

→ *Assess.*
What's in the tank? Draw an arrow to how full your energy tank is right now.

½

E   F

→ *Recharge.*
Something I am grateful for today:

_____

_____

Someone I am grateful for today:

_____

_____

One piece of advice I'd give a teammate if they were in my situation:

_____

_____

→ *Visualize.* Spend a few minutes imagining your favorite sports play. This can be a moment when you were your happiest, most fulfilled or having an amazing game. The key here is to choose a moment where you were doing something well. Add as much detail as possible including sights, sounds, emotions, colors, etc.

_____ / _____ / _____

"The process of it drives me to come back. I want to see if I can. I don't know if I can. I want to find out,"

-Kobe Bryant on his achilles injury.

Some comparisons can actually be good for you. For example, when you compare values (things on the inside) it can motivate you to do your own value work, too. Read APPENDIX B when you finish this day.

Write down the name of someone you **admire** or who **inspires** and **motivates** you:

_____

WHY do they inspire you?

_____

_____

_____

WHAT kind of person are they?
WHAT kind of qualities do they have?

_____

_____

PRO TIP: Write an "I am" statement (like the ones from the appendix) about your values.

_____

PRIME TIME

➡ *Assess.*

What's in the tank? Draw an arrow to how full your energy tank is right now.

E   ½   F

➡ *Recharge.*

Something I am grateful for today:

_____

_____

Someone I am grateful for today:

_____

_____

One piece of advice I'd give a teammate if they were in my situation:

_____

_____

➡ *Visualize.* Spend a few minutes imagining your favorite sports play. This can be a moment when you were your happiest, most fulfilled or having an amazing game. The key here is to choose a moment where you were doing something well. Add as much detail as possible including sights, sounds, emotions, colors, etc.

___ / ___ / ___

Self-talk isn't just for the court, it's for everywhere. We need good habits for self-communication.

What are some things I say to myself when I compare my progress to another athlete?

_____

_____

_____

_____

_____

Are these things

 **Helpful** TO MY PROGRESS

 **Not so helpful** TO MY PROGRESS

PRO TIP: Each day, each moment is an opportunity to learn something about yourself. Say this to yourself:
"My progress is my progress. I get out what I put in."

Write this down and put it somewhere that you can see it daily.

PRIME TIME

➡ *Assess.*
What's in the tank? Draw an arrow to how full your energy tank is right now.

➡ *Recharge.*
Something I am grateful for today:

_____

_____

Someone I am grateful for today:

_____

_____

One piece of advice I'd give a teammate if they were in my situation:

_____

_____

➡ *Visualize.* Spend a few minutes imagining your favorite sports play. This can be a moment when you were your happiest, most fulfilled or having an amazing game. The key here is to choose a moment where you were doing something well. Add as much detail as possible including sights, sounds, emotions, colors, etc.

/ /

WEEKLY RECAP - THE TRAP

Write down **three** ways comparison has derailed my progress in the past:

_____

_____

_____

Two new tools I learned in this section that will keep me focused on my progress.

_____

_____

One strong emotion I felt this week and how I learned from it

_____

PRO TIP: Have a conversation with someone who inspires you. Ask them who they look up to and why.

THE WORK

Mental Reps

There's no easy way around the work. When you are injured, sometimes you can't get the physical reps like you are used to getting. Here's where you up your mental game. In this section you will learn some tools for imagery and visualization. Your brain can do amazing things when you rehearse not only skills, but emotions. It's basically free reps if you are willing to do the work.

PRIME TIME

➡ *Assess.*
What's in the tank? Draw an arrow to how full your energy tank is right now.

➡ *Recharge.*
Something I am grateful for today:

_____

_____

Someone I am grateful for today:

_____

_____

One piece of advice I'd give a teammate if they were in my situation:

_____

_____

➡ *Visualize.* Spend a few minutes imagining your favorite sports play. This can be a moment when you were your happiest, most fulfilled or having an amazing game. The key here is to choose a moment where you were doing something well. Add as much detail as possible including sights, sounds, emotions, colors, etc.

When you cannot physically perform a skill or "see" the ending you want for yourself, you can visualize or imagine what the story may look like.

Visualization is mental rehearsal for a particular skill or aspect of your game. Read APPENDIX A before completing this day.

What is **one skill** I want to rehearse in my mind?

_____

_____

What is **one aspect** of my game I want to rehearse?

_____

_____

Why did I pick these?

_____

_____

❙ PRO TIP: If you skipped your visualization for today, DO IT NOW.

PRIME TIME

➜ *Assess.*
What's in the tank? Draw an arrow to how full your energy tank is right now.

➜ *Recharge.*
Something I am grateful for today:

_____

_____

Someone I am grateful for today:

_____

_____

One piece of advice I'd give a teammate if they were in my situation:

_____

_____

➜ *Visualize.* Spend a few minutes imagining your favorite sports play. This can be a moment when you were your happiest, most fulfilled or having an amazing game. The key here is to choose a moment where you were doing something well. Add as much detail as possible including sights, sounds, emotions, colors, etc.

_____ / _____ / _____

"The key to effective visualization is to create the most detailed, clear and vivid a picture to focus on."

–Georges St-Pierre

The **best place** for me to try or practice visualization is:

_____

The **best time of day** for me to practice visualization is:

_____

_____

PRO TIP: You can also visualize long-term goals. Write down one of your long term goals.

_____

_____

PRIME TIME

➜ *Assess.*
What's in the tank? Draw an arrow to how full your energy tank is right now.

½

E   F

⊙

➜ *Recharge.*
Something I am grateful for today:

_____

_____

Someone I am grateful for today:

_____

_____

One piece of advice I'd give a teammate if they were in my situation:

_____

_____

➜ *Visualize.* Spend a few minutes imagining your favorite sports play. This can be a moment when you were your happiest, most fulfilled or having an amazing game. The key here is to choose a moment where you were doing something well. Add as much detail as possible including sights, sounds, emotions, colors, etc.

__ / __ / __

Effective visualization must be positive – meaning, you must visualize yourself doing the skill well or making the winning point.

Fill in the blanks using as much detail as possible and considering all your senses:

When I VISUALIZE this skill:

What do I *hear*?_____

_____

Who or what do I *see*?_____

_____

What do I *feel*?_____

_____

Where in my body do I *feel* this emotion?_____

_____

Who am I *playing for*?_____

_____

PRIME TIME

➜ *Assess.*
What's in the tank? Draw an arrow to how full your energy tank is right now.

½

E   F

➜ *Recharge.*
Something I am grateful for today:

_____

_____

Someone I am grateful for today:

_____

_____

One piece of advice I'd give a teammate if they were in my situation:

_____

_____

➜ *Visualize.* Spend a few minutes imagining your favorite sports play. This can be a moment when you were your happiest, most fulfilled or having an amazing game. The key here is to choose a moment where you were doing something well. Add as much detail as possible including sights, sounds, emotions, colors, etc.

_/_ _/_

"*I never think about a play or visualize anything. I do what comes to me at the moment. Instinct. It has always been that way,*"

-Lionel Messi

Think about the quote above:

☐ **I agree with the quote**

☐ **I disagree with the quote**

☐ **I neither agree nor disagree with the quote**

Why did you answer the way you did?

_____

_____

_____

_____

_____

PRIME TIME

→ *Assess.*
What's in the tank? Draw an arrow to how full your energy tank is right now.

½

E   F

→ *Recharge.*
Something I am grateful for today:

_____

_____

Someone I am grateful for today:

_____

_____

One piece of advice I'd give a teammate if they were in my situation:

_____

_____

→ *Visualize.* Spend a few minutes imagining your favorite sports play. This can be a moment when you were your happiest, most fulfilled or having an amazing game. The key here is to choose a moment where you were doing something well. Add as much detail as possible including sights, sounds, emotions, colors, etc.

"I really think a champion is defined not by their wins, but by how they can recover when they fall."

-Serena Williams

Mental reps, like physical reps, take practice – they are part of your work. It is important to schedule time in your day to work on mental skills or performance work like visualization and journaling.

Make a commitment to arriving to rehab or physical therapy ten minutes early and set an intention for you work. Fill in the following commitment card:

On this day _____, I will commit to
　　　　　　　　　(day/date)

arriving to my rehab or PT session _____ minutes

early to visualize a particular skill or to set an intention for my

time. My intentional goal is _____
　　　　　　　　　　　　(pick a goal or intention to focus on)

_____ and I will ask my trainer or PT _____
　　　　　　　　　　　　　　　　(trainer or P.T name)

_____ to hold me accountable for this intention

because this work and my return to play is important to me.

_____　　　_____
(trainer initials)　　　　　*(my signature)*

PRIME TIME

➜ *Assess.*
What's in the tank? Draw an arrow to how full your energy tank is right now.

➜ *Recharge.*
Something I am grateful for today:

_____

_____

Someone I am grateful for today:

_____

_____

One piece of advice I'd give a teammate if they were in my situation:

_____

_____

➜ *Visualize.* Spend a few minutes imagining your favorite sports play. This can be a moment when you were your happiest, most fulfilled or having an amazing game. The key here is to choose a moment where you were doing something well. Add as much detail as possible including sights, sounds, emotions, colors, etc.

"A legacy is built by more than what is seen. It is not given, it is earned."

-Michael Jordan

Imagine the day you return to your sport.

What does that look like?
Write the story below.

MY NAME

PRIME TIME

➡️ *Assess.*
What's in the tank? Draw an arrow to how full your energy tank is right now.

½

E   F

⊙

➡️ *Recharge.*
Something I am grateful for today:

_____

_____

Someone I am grateful for today:

_____

_____

One piece of advice I'd give a teammate if they were in my situation:

_____

_____

➡️ *Visualize.* Spend a few minutes imagining your favorite sports play. This can be a moment when you were your happiest, most fulfilled or having an amazing game. The key here is to choose a moment where you were doing something well. Add as much detail as possible including sights, sounds, emotions, colors, etc.

WEEKLY RECAP – THE WORK

"At first it was really devastating, but I think it also allowed me time to refocus my mentality and my goals,"

-Julie Ertz, United States Women's National Team

You are finishing up three weeks of a NEW HABIT! Think back to week one.

How has journaling daily helped you refocus your mentality?

How has it kept you focused on your own progress and your goals?

_____

_____

_____

_____

_____

_____

_____

THE SHIFT

"I am <u>NOT</u> the <u>SAME</u> athlete!"

It's all in how you say that statement above. If you say it without emphasis on any particular word, it can sound defeating. When you say the same statement with the emphasis on the words in all caps above, you give yourself power to change the story. You are not defined by your injury or any setback. You are not defined by your sport. You are defined by your work and how you choose to rise today.

PRIME TIME

➡️ *Assess.*
What's in the tank? Draw an arrow to how full your energy tank is right now.

½

E   F

⊙

➡️ *Recharge.*
Something I am grateful for today:

_____

_____

Someone I am grateful for today:

_____

_____

One piece of advice I'd give a teammate if they were in my situation:

_____

_____

➡️ *Visualize.* Spend a few minutes imagining your favorite sports play. This can be a moment when you were your happiest, most fulfilled or having an amazing game. The key here is to choose a moment where you were doing something well. Add as much detail as possible including sights, sounds, emotions, colors, etc.

"We have to have the mentality that we have to work for everything we're going to get."

-Steph Curry

Getting sidelined by an injury is never something we plan for, but it forces us to take a step back and adjust our mindset and attitude.

T   **F**   Being sidelined changes my identity as an athlete

T   **F**   Being sidelined reminds me how much I still love playing sports

T   **F**   Being sidelined makes me work harder for my goals

T   **F**   Being sidelined taught me that mental skills are as important as physical skills

T   **F**   Being sidelined is an opportunity to learn, not a final ending

T   **F**   I am excited to see what's possible when I return to play

PRIME TIME

➡️ *Assess.*
What's in the tank? Draw an arrow to how full your energy tank is right now.

➡️ *Recharge.*
Something I am grateful for today:

_____

_____

Someone I am grateful for today:

_____

_____

One piece of advice I'd give a teammate if they were in my situation:

_____

_____

➡️ *Visualize.* Spend a few minutes imagining your favorite sports play. This can be a moment when you were your happiest, most fulfilled or having an amazing game. The key here is to choose a moment where you were doing something well. Add as much detail as possible including sights, sounds, emotions, colors, etc.

"As a competitor, you want to get on the field as soon as you can. But you want to do what's best for your team, your career and everything. That's not up to me to decide,"

-Carson Wentz

When you return to the field, or pitch, or pool deck, or court, **you will not be the same athlete** as before. You will be:

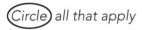 all that apply

CONFIDENT	MENTALLY TOUGHER
CAUTIOUS	PHYSICALLY TOUGHER
SMARTER	GRATEFUL
EFFICIENT	BETTER TEAMMATE
FEARFUL	OPEN TO LEARNING
LEADER	MORE DETERMINED

My **new perspective** is:

_____

_____

_____

PRIME TIME

➜ *Assess.*
What's in the tank? Draw an arrow to how full your energy tank is right now.

½

E   F

⊙

➜ *Recharge.*
Something I am grateful for today:

_____

_____

Someone I am grateful for today:

_____

_____

One piece of advice I'd give a teammate if they were in my situation:

_____

_____

➜ *Visualize.* Spend a few minutes imagining your favorite sports play. This can be a moment when you were your happiest, most fulfilled or having an amazing game. The key here is to choose a moment where you were doing something well. Add as much detail as possible including sights, sounds, emotions, colors, etc.

___ / ___ / ___

"I came back from my ACL injury and won MVP. So what's a groin? What's an adductor? That's how I look at things [now],"

-Adrian Peterson

⭐ **What** is my **biggest motivation** for getting healthy?

_____

_____

_____

_____

⭐ **Who** is my **biggest motivation** or who inspires me to keep pressing forward every day?

_____

_____

_____

_____

PRIME TIME

➡️ *Assess.*
What's in the tank? Draw an arrow to how full your energy tank is right now.

➡️ *Recharge.*
Something I am grateful for today:

_____

_____

Someone I am grateful for today:

_____

_____

One piece of advice I'd give a teammate if they were in my situation:

_____

_____

➡️ *Visualize.* Spend a few minutes imagining your favorite sports play. This can be a moment when you were your happiest, most fulfilled or having an amazing game. The key here is to choose a moment where you were doing something well. Add as much detail as possible including sights, sounds, emotions, colors, etc.

Think about the people close to you who have had your back since you got injured. Write their names and some character trait or attribute about them in the space below.

Name:

_____

Attribute

_____

Name:

_____

Attribute

_____

Name:

_____

Attribute

_____

Name:

_____

Attribute

_____

PRIME TIME

➤ *Assess.*
What's in the tank? Draw an arrow to how full your energy tank is right now.

½

E   F

➤ *Recharge.*
Something I am grateful for today:

_____

_____

Someone I am grateful for today:

_____

_____

One piece of advice I'd give a teammate if they were in my situation:

_____

_____

➤ *Visualize.* Spend a few minutes imagining your favorite sports play. This can be a moment when you were your happiest, most fulfilled or having an amazing game. The key here is to choose a moment where you were doing something well. Add as much detail as possible including sights, sounds, emotions, colors, etc.

"There's a lot of pressure on me, but I don't put a lot of pressure on myself. I feel if I play my game it will take care of itself,"

-LeBron James

Do you have or do you put pressure on yourself?

○ **yes**

○ **no**

If yes, in what way?

_____

_____

_____

Is this pressure helpful to your recovery process? Why or why not?

_____

_____

_____

PRIME TIME

➡ *Assess.*
What's in the tank? Draw an arrow to how full your energy tank is right now.

➡ *Recharge.*
Something I am grateful for today:

_____

_____

Someone I am grateful for today:

_____

_____

One piece of advice I'd give a teammate if they were in my situation:

_____

_____

➡ *Visualize.* Spend a few minutes imagining your favorite sports play. This can be a moment when you were your happiest, most fulfilled or having an amazing game. The key here is to choose a moment where you were doing something well. Add as much detail as possible including sights, sounds, emotions, colors, etc.

DAY **27**

___ / ___ / ___

Cue words or mantras are short repeated words or sayings that can be used to relax or remind you why you play and why you are working to get back to competing.

It can be a quote, scripture or a series of words that are meaningful to you. **Write your cue word** or mantra on the sticky notes below.

ex: "I don't need easy, I just need possible,"
-Bethany Hamilton

PRO TIP: Write one of yours on a sticky note, notecard, or put it in your phone where you will see it daily.

PRIME TIME

➡ *Assess.*
What's in the tank? Draw an arrow to how full your energy tank is right now.

➡ *Recharge.*
Something I am grateful for today:

_____

_____

Someone I am grateful for today:

_____

_____

One piece of advice I'd give a teammate if they were in my situation:

_____

_____

➡ *Visualize.* Spend a few minutes imagining your favorite sports play. This can be a moment when you were your happiest, most fulfilled or having an amazing game. The key here is to choose a moment where you were doing something well. Add as much detail as possible including sights, sounds, emotions, colors, etc.

DAY **28**

_____ / _____ / _____

WEEKLY RECAP – THE SHIFT

You just finished 30 days of creating, establishing or sharpening habits and skills that will train and level up your mental game.

Write a thank you note to yourself showing your gratitude for sticking to your mental training and seeing this habit through. Use the "notes" pages at the back of this journal if you need more room.

Now that you've completed your 30 days of journaling, re-rate yourself for each question using the scale below. Did any of your scores change? If so, what and why?

1   **2**   **3**   **4**

nope   *meh*   *sometimes*   *100%*

I journal regularly   _____

I believe journaling is a valuable mental skill   _____

I am open to feedback   _____

I apply feedback well   _____

I ask questions to learn   _____

I believe the mental game is as important   _____
as the physical game

I work hard on my mental game   _____

I have been told I "get in my head"   _____

I get down on myself as an athlete   _____

I bounce back after setbacks and mistakes   _____

My coach inspires and motivates me   _____

Congratulations on completing the **30 DAY RETURN TO PLAY Journal**! I hope you discovered some valuable tools to use not only as you return to play, but to build on as you continue your career as an athlete. Remember, you train your mind like you train your muscles, by consistently building new skills every day.

Mindset skills don't happen overnight, like everything else in sports, they take practice and persistence. The more tools we have when we play, the more tools we'll have when we aren't playing. It's not something we talk about often, but every athlete's journey comes to an end. Some of us get long careers through high school, club, college, even professional playing time but every athlete's journey does end – yes, even yours. The highest performers know this and maximize their time in the arena every chance they get and leverage their experience once they are done.

Priscilla Tallman
MS, Clinical Psychology

Share your feedback!

email: pytallman@gmail.com
website: www.spikedr.com

30 DAY RESET JOURNAL

Don't let your progress stop here, continue your work with **The 30 Day RESET Journal**. Most athletes know the mental aspect of their game is important, but few of them know how to train it. The **30 Day RESET Journal** helps create and establish new habits for journaling, gratitude, self-awareness and more. For four weeks, athletes learn to define their mindset, create better systems for goal setting, be aware of distractions, learn

self and other communication skills and how to take responsibility for their athletic performance. This journal isn't just a tool for athletes, it's also an important resource for coaches, athletic trainers, sports med, physical therapists and parents or volunteers who work closely with athletes.

"This mindset program has fortified previous habits as well as equipped me with plenty of additional tools and strategies to attack the next chapter of my life. As I go into college and another season of competition, I am confident in my new abilities to bounce back quickly, hanclle pressure, anct be a true competitor. Priscilla is an amazing listener and is extremely knowledgeable and helpful."

-A. Johnson, Mindset Journaling Athlete

Information for this appendix has been compiled and created as a source for client education in a clinical setting and may contain research and references from "Social Psychology" by David G Myers & Jean M Twenge.

This appendix is not a diagnostic tool. If you or someone you know have a life threatening situation or need immediate medical help, call your doctor or dial 911.

APPENDIX A: Visualization

What is visualization?

Visualization (or imagery) is a tool used by many athletes to rehearse a certain sport, skill or emotion for a future sporting event. Skill specific visualization helps sharpen a desired change in a skill while emotional visualization rehearses a big emotion or prepares our bodies for stressful or overwhelming situations.

Why is visualization important?

Visualization is important because we cannot rehearse a certain event before we are actually there – unless we rehearse the scenario in our minds. For sport specific skills, visualization creates new brain connections without having to physically perform the skill – it's free reps. You still need to train and practice physically, but visualization is another way to perform the skill.

How do I visualize?

- Find a quiet place and set aside five minutes to work through a particular skill or scenario in your mind. Close your eyes and imagine what you want to work on.

- Add as much sensory detail as you possibly can. Think of your five senses: sight, smell, sound, taste, touch and add how you are feeling.

- If you are feeling anxious, where in your body do you feel anxious? Rehearse that feeling, then replace the anxiety with a feeling of confidence or overcoming. See yourself turning from being anxious and overwhelmed to confident and prepared.

- One main key of visualization is to see yourself performing the skill well or successfully.

- Take a few deep breaths and open your eyes.

APPENDIX B: IDENTITY VS VALUES

"What You Do" versus "Who You Are"

Athlete IDENTITY	Athlete VALUE
Athlete identity is what sport we play and what we do as athletes.	Values are the internal operating system by which we live our lives.
Your athlete identity is defined by how you perceive yourself and how others perceive you as an athlete. **Identity is external.**	Your values are defined by (but not limited to) culture, religion, ethnicity, community, sport played, family, etc. **Values are internal.**
We identify as part of an athletic community, sports program or particular team.	You make decisions based on your values every single day. To make better decisions, know your values.
Your athlete identity is what you do. **"I am an athlete."**	Your values as an athlete are who you are. **"I am driven, determined and hard-working."**

APPENDIX C: DEPRESSION

What are the symptoms of depression?

- Depressed mood or sadness most of the time

- Lack of energy

- Inability to enjoy things that used to bring pleasure

- Withdrawal from friends and family

- Irritability, anger, or anxiety

- Inability to concentrate

- Significant weight loss or gain

- Significant change in sleep patterns (inability to fall asleep, stay asleep, or get up in the morning)

- Feelings of guilt or worthlessness

- Aches and pains (with no known medical cause)

- Pessimism and indifference (not caring about anything in the present or future)

- Thoughts of death or suicide

When someone has five or more of these symptoms more often than not for two weeks or longer, that person is probably depressed.

How is depression different from regular sadness?

Everyone has some ups and downs, and sadness is a natural emotion. The normal stresses of life can lead anyone to feel sad every once in a while. Things like an argument with a friend or spouse, loss of a job, life transitions such as moving or getting a new job or starting a new school, not being chosen for a team, or a best friend moving out of town can lead to feelings of sadness, disappointment, or grief. These reactions are usually brief and go away with a little time and care.

Depression is more than occasionally feeling blue, sad, or down in the dumps, though. Depression is a strong mood involving sadness, discouragement, despair, or hopelessness that lasts for an extended period of time. It interferes with a person's ability to participate in normal activities.

Depression affects a person's thoughts, outlook, and behavior as well as mood. In addition to a depressed mood, a person with depression may feel tired, irritable, and notice changes in appetite. When someone has depression, it can cloud everything. The world looks bleak and the person's thoughts reflect that hopelessness. Depression tends to create negative and self-critical thoughts. Because of feelings of sadness and low energy, those with depression may pull away from those around them or from activities they once enjoyed. This usually makes them feel more lonely and isolated, worsening their condition. Depression can be mild or severe. At its worst, depression can create such feelings of despair that a person contemplates suicide.

Why does one become depressed?

There is no single cause for depression. Many factors play a role including genetics, life events, family and social environment and medical conditions.

Genetics: Research shows that some individuals inherit genes that make it more likely for them to get depressed. However, not everyone who has the genetic makeup for depression becomes depressed, and many who have no family history of depression have the condition.

Life Events: The death of a family member, friend, or pet can sometimes go beyond normal grief and lead to depression. Other difficult life events, such as when parents divorce, separate, or remarry, can trigger depression. Even events like moving or changing schools can be emotionally challenging enough that a person becomes depressed.

Family and Social Environment: A negative, stressful, or unhappy family atmosphere can have a negative effect on one's self-esteem and lead to depression. This can also include high-stress living situations such as poverty, homelessness, or violence. Substance abuse could cause chemical changes in the brain that negatively impact mood. The damaging social and personal consequences of substance abuse can also lead to depression.

Medical Conditions: Certain medical conditions can affect hormone balance and therefore lead to depression. When these medical conditions are diagnosed and treated by a doctor, the depression usually disappears. For some, undiagnosed learning disabilities might block school, work or relationship success, hormonal changes might affect mood, or physical illnesses might present challenges or setbacks.

How do I get help?

Depression is one of the most common emotional problems around the world. The good news is that it's also one of the most treatable conditions. Those who get help for their depression have a better quality of life and enjoy themselves in ways that they weren't able to before.

APPENDIX C

Treatment for depression can include psychotherapy, medication, or a combination of both. Psychotherapy with a mental health professional is very effective in treating depression. Therapy sessions can help one understand more about why they feel depressed and learn ways to combat it. Sometimes, doctors prescribe medicine for a patient with depression. It can take a few weeks before that person feels the medicine working. Because every person's brain is different, what works well for one person might not work for another.

Everyone can benefit from mood-boosting activities like exercise, yoga, dance, journaling, or art. It can also help to keep busy no matter how tired you feel.

Those who are depressed shouldn't wait around hoping it will go away on its own; depression can be effectively treated. Others may need to step in if someone seems severely depressed and isn't getting help.

Many find that it helps to open up to others including friends, family or other individuals they trust. Simply saying, "I've been feeling really down lately and I think I'm depressed," can be a good way to begin the discussion. Ask to arrange an appointment with a therapist. For teens, if a parent or family member can't help, turn to a school counselor, best friend, or a helpline.

APPENDIX D: ANXIETY

Introduction to Anxiety

Generalized Anxiety Disorder or GAD is characterized by excessive, exaggerated anxiety about everyday life events. People with symptoms of GAD tend to always expect disaster and can't stop worrying about health, money, family, work, or school. These worries are often unrealistic or out of proportion for the situation. Daily life becomes a constant state of unease, fear, and dread. Eventually, the anxiety so dominates the person's thinking that it interferes with daily functioning.

What is anxiety?

Anxiety is a natural human reaction that serves an important basic survival function. It acts as an alarm system that is activated whenever a person perceives danger. When the body reacts to a potential threat, a person feels physical sensations of anxiety: a faster heartbeat and breath rate, tensed muscles, sweaty palms, nausea, and trembling hands or legs. These sensations are part of the body's fight-flight response, which is caused by a rush of adrenaline and other chemicals. This reaction prepares the body to make a quick decision to either stay and fight that threat or try to escape from it (fight or flight). It takes a few seconds longer for the thinking part of the brain (the cortex) to process the situation and evaluate whether the threat is real, and if it is, how to handle it. If the cortex sends the all-clear signal, the fight-flight response is deactivated and the nervous system can relax. If the brain reasons that a threat might last, feelings of anxiety and the physical symptoms listed above may linger, keeping the person alert.

APPENDIX **D**

What are the symptoms of generalized anxiety disorder?

GAD affects the way a person thinks, but the anxiety can lead to physical symptoms as well. Symptoms of GAD include:

- Excessive, ongoing worry and tension
- An unrealistic view of problems
- Restlessness or a feeling of being "edgy"
- Irritability
- Muscle tension
- Headaches
- Sweating
- Difficulty concentrating
- Nausea
- The need to go to the bathroom frequently
- Tiredness
- Trouble falling or staying asleep
- Trembling
- Being easily startled
- Other anxiety disorders (such as panic disorder, obsessive-compulsive disorder and phobias)
- Depression
- Drug/alcohol abuse

What causes generalized anxiety disorder?

Although the exact cause of GAD is not known, a number of factors, including genetics, brain chemistry, and environmental stressors appear to contribute to its development.

Genetics: Some research suggests that family history plays a part in increasing the likelihood that a person will develop GAD. This means that the tendency to develop GAD may be passed on in families.

Brain chemistry: GAD has been associated with abnormal levels of certain neurotransmitters in the brain. Neurotransmitters are special chemical messengers that help move information between nerve cells. If the neurotransmitters are out of balance, messages cannot travel through the brain properly. This can alter the way the brain reacts in certain situations, leading to anxiety.

Environmental factors: Trauma and stressful events, such as abuse, the death of a loved one, divorce, or changing jobs or schools may lead to GAD. The use of and withdrawal from addictive substances, including alcohol, caffeine, and nicotine, could also worsen anxiety.

How are anxiety disorders treated?

Anxiety disorders can be treated by both mental health professionals and therapists. A therapist can look at the symptoms someone is dealing with, diagnose the specific anxiety disorder, and create a plan to help the person get relief. A particular type of talk therapy called cognitive-behavior therapy (CBT) is often used. In CBT, a person learns new ways to think and act in situations that can cause anxiety, and to manage and deal with stress. The therapist provides support and guidance and teaches new coping skills such as relaxation techniques or breathing exercises. Sometimes, but not always, medication is used as part of the treatment for anxiety.

How common is generalized anxiety disorder?

About 4 million American adults suffer from GAD during the course of a year. It most often begins in childhood or adolescence, but can begin in adulthood. It is more common in women than in men.

APPENDIX E: HEALTHY COPING

Distracting ourselves when things are stressful or sad or over-whelming can be a healthy way to cope, but sometimes the same distraction can lead to unhealthy coping or numbing out.

DISTRACTIONS

Distractions are people, places or activities that prevent us from giving full attention to something or someone else. When they keep us from getting something done or meeting a goal, dis-tractions are not helpful. When we need a mini-vacation from work, play or from a stressful situation, distractions can be a helpful way to reset our focus. So, how do we choose?

HEALTHY COPING

A coping mechanism is something we do to tolerate or mini-mize stress or unwanted emotions. Healthy coping may include exercise, eating nutritious foods, spending time with friends or loved ones, journaling, being in nature, resting, meditating, listening to music, etc. Healthy coping will bring us CLOSER in relationship with ourselves or others. Can you think of some other healthy coping strategies?

UNHEALTHY COPING

Unhealthy coping PUSHES US AWAY from relationships with ourself or others. Unhealthy coping examples are alcohol or drug abuse, toxic relationships or friendships, abusive relation-ships, comparing on social media, controlling or blaming others. It can be a substance, a person or a behavior.

APPENDIX **E**

NUMBING OUT OR SELF-MEDICATING

If unhealthy coping pushes us away, numbing out and self-medicating ISOLATE US from ourselves or others. These are behaviors, people or substances designed to numb feelings. The problem is when you numb out the unwanted feelings, you numb out the good ones you need too - leading to further isolation.

HEALTHY COPING BREEDS CONNECTION

Connecting with others and sharing our thoughts and feelings might be the best way to cope and connect. However, when we cannot physically connect with others, it's important we still find healthy ways to connect with our own process, emotions and thoughts.

Notes

---- Notes ----

Notes

Priscilla Tallman works with athletes as a Performance Mindset Coach. Tallman's athletic career includes First Team All-America honors and First Team All-SEC honors all four years at the University of Georgia including Freshman of the Year in 1991 and Player of the Year in 1994. Tallman also played two tours with the USA National Team in 1994 and 1995 and a year of professional volleyball in Geneva, Switzerland. In 2006 she was inducted into the University of Georgia's prestigious Circle of Honor.

Tallman has an undergraduate degree in Psychology and a Master of Science Degree in Clinical Psychology. She is active as a coach in youth sports and local club sports and has coached Beach Volleyball in the PAC-12. Her passion is to raise, train and teach athletes mindset skills that will give them an edge in their sport and habits for life.

She is also a writer and has been published in Volleyball Magazine, SweatRX, The Art of Coaching Volleyball and writes personal essays about coaching, sports culture and mental health in student-athlete populations.

www.spikedr.com

 @pytallman

 pytallman@gmail.com